East

West

and Beyond

East West and Beyond

Gloria Dyc

Plain View Press
P. O. 42255
Austin, TX 78704

plainviewpress.net
sbright1@austin.rr.com
1-512-440-7139

Copyright Gloria Dyc, 2007. All rights reserved.
ISBN: 978-1-891386-59-6
Library of Congress Number: 2006938136

Cover photo by Milan Sklenar, "Mother Pinon"
Back photo by Judy David

Acknowledgements

Some of these poems appeared originally in *48222: A Detroit Book of Poetry*, *The Spirit that Moves Us*, *Sing! Heavenly Muse*, *Horizons: An Anthology of South Dakota Writers*, *Plainswoman*, *Moving Out*, *The South Dakota Review*, *Passages North*, *Wanbli Ho*, *The White Clouds Review*, *The Midland Review*, *The Taos Review*, *The Painted Bride Quarterly*, *Red Mesa Review*, *Earth's Daughters*, *Contact II*, and *Prairie Schooner*.

*May all beings in the east
and all beings in the west
be liberated into the beyond…*

Contents

East   9

> [Three days after the blizzard]   11
> Vernal Equinox   12
> Cargo of Grace   13
> Foolish Young Woman, Careless Cruel Man   14
> [November and still the river]   15
> Language Barrier   16
> Portrait of my Mother in the Year of My Birth   17
> The Seminole Who Wrestled Alligators   18
> While Gardening, I Remember a Dream   19
> Primal Dream   20

West   23

> The Hitch-hiker   25
> Paying Attention   27
> Thinning the Herd   29
> Heart of Clover   31
> Picking Tea in Grass Mountain   32
> Lament for the Waning Female Moons   33
> Alice Fish at a Rosebud **Wacipi**   **34**
> Gladys Makes Room for Them Crosses Over   36
> Somehow We Managed   38
> Agnes, Trying to Stay Sober   39
> Dreams in a Season of Drought   41
> In Honor of the **Wakinyan Oyate**   **43**
> On the Fourth Day   44
> Dream of Purification   46

Beyond   47

> Locating Myself in Space and Time   49
> Spirit of the Horse   51
> Circle of Wildness   52
> Meditations on Water in the Desert   53

Exhumation of Florence C. Lister, author of
        Anazazi Pottery   55
Visit to a Chaco Canyon Excavation   57
A Storm, A Dream   58
Land-owner   59
We Create Myth   61
Love at Mid-Life   65
Continental Divide   68
The Return of Odysseus   69
Holy Rain   70
Gathering Poles at Quaking Aspens   72

About the Author   75

East

Three days after the blizzard
a grouse appeared to us
on the bank near the railroad
Behind the sun was so brilliant
the bird had the aura of a saint
We stopped the car a moment
the bird stood like you do when
half-dressed you realize
I am watching you from the next room
then the bird scuttled off for camouflage
I am thinking of this beauty now
not so uncommon yet startling when
most cars remained landlocked
and we worried about the weight
of the snow on our roofs
You are like the grouse to me, I say
we are listening to Art Tatum
and the day is rolling away
sheet music on a player piano
You want to know how
when you come closer I can sense
from the river nearby great slabs of ice
beginning to shift after hours of sun
and soon we begin to navigate like fish
through this darkness and this bliss

Vernal Equinox

This is like watching
a photograph develop
but in reverse
Slowly I am losing the contrast
between the pines and snow
Lake Michigan recedes in darkness
each wave breaking new
as an infant's first breath
I am singular in this eclipse
at ease on these rented sheets
my breath familiar as
steam from a kettle
My lover opens the door
without knocking
He wants to knows something
about broiling a steak
Ah, sweet fall from paradise
he cooks his own food
I reach for the lamp
when I am left alone with the negative
There is such distance that
later I resort to a letter
He responds by escorting me to the door
where we can watch by porch light
large flakes of snow covering
our tracks in the driveway

Cargo of Grace

Finally the ships return to the river
I'd almost given up hope this long winter
they signal to me in their baritone
adding resonance to the most mundane acts
Only a month ago the icy banks lost their moorings
and I read of a dog rescued from a floe
by two men with compassion and a canoe in storage
Often I've imagined the shock of the cold water to the dog
how quickly he must have relinquished the image of a bird
as he struggled that evening for a footing
And I've imagined the curious light in his eyes
as he might have turned for a moment from his rescuers
to the terrible vacuum that would have been his
Now the congestion of the lakes has been conveyed down
a river the color of an eel
a river relentless and austere as a plant
Finally the ships return and signal to me
I reel to the banks as if stunned by fever
greedily I unload their cargo of grace

Foolish Young Woman, Careless Cruel Man

I was still a twig and dreamy
easily seduced by the professor
who slipped a chapbook of poetry
under my apartment door
To his semester-end soiree
I wore an antique velvet dress
blonde hair draped over my breasts
I drank cheap champagne
with the other girls who came
How we laughed; our young men
deferred in the shadows

He came to my apartment
with daffodils one noon
and asked me about birth control
as he unbuckled his pants
He came quite quickly
then in the bathroom soaped
his offending cock and said
"This is the best part"
I was confused, but honored

Then his wife appeared on the stairs
and a fog descended on us
She asked us to keep our voices down
so as not to awaken the baby
he hadn't told us about that
And I thought: How old she is!
circles under her eyes
the thickness of her waist!
And when he came to me again
glimpsing at pages of my poetry
I thought he would see some truth
finally, but he put them quickly aside
and asked if we had time and privacy
I was such a foolish young woman
and he was such a careless cruel man

November and still the river

flowed free of ice
It was dark that Saturday
when I went through the back door of the butcher's
the routine shopping at hand
A few feet from the door a skinned carcass
almost slapped me in the face
With its slender legs and tapered body
this wasn't a steer
One of the butchers smiled and tossed
the head of the deer in a box
I looked about: I was in a morgue
to my left a butcher worked diligently
separating the flesh from bone with a knife
Most people want to keep the hide
At my feet laid another deer
eyes, hooves, antlers perfect and intact
but the chest of the deer had been hollowed
I stared at the clean cavity
and I nudged the deer with my boot
to drive a nail of reality into my skull
This was two weeks after the abortion
that day I carried the heart of the deer
like a stone beneath my tongue
and the word *nothing*
was a feather in my throat

Language Barrier

My grandmother spoke little English
"Come and eat" was a phrase she knew
my father advised us not to refuse
an invitation to her table
"Teach them the language," my mother urged
even his silence could not be translated
The air was an intoxicating broth
of sausage, cabbage, and feathers
As she sat and talked in Polish
vines of language grew between us
lush as the concord grapes on her fence
Often she appeared critical and angry
but then she would laugh and shrug
We knew very little about her
even the length of her hair
which she kept harnessed in a bun
posed a mystery for us
My mother resented the way
she tested for dust on her visits
running a finger along dresser tops
She worked very hard on her acre
cultivating flowers, corn, and raspberries
and slept deep in a feather bed
On the wall was a photo of my grandfather
retouched with pastels in an oval frame
a man we never met: the family secret
a man who had shot himself in the basement
How were we to judge this woman
who dishonored her husband with a child
conceived in Poland while he labored
in an American coal mine for an acre of land?
Her stockings were opaque and salmon-colored
We had to accept the flesh beneath on faith

Portrait of my Mother
in the Year of my Birth

She is ironing in the damp basement
grease from the tool and die shop
rises off the steamy plaid shirt
He is away at work and these hours
are hers free of arguments and strain
Pregnant again and he acting ***that way***
she watches the McCarthy trials
Divorce Court and then Queen for a Day
She weeps along with the widow
who has lost her home in a fire
and feels again the injustices of life
One of her brothers has become
a millionaire by selling Chevrolets
the other, a Jesuit, solemnly proclaims
God only gives a cross to those
strong enough to bear it
She is advised: novenas and compliance
cold water on the face and a nice dinner
on Fridays she grates potatoes and onions
as her mother-in-law did
and cries over the irritation
and her unnamed sin

The Seminole Who Wrestled Alligators

Before we crossed the Mackinaw Bridge
and entered the wilderness of the U.P.
our family toured Sea Shell City
to watch a man who wrestled alligators
The store was infused with a tropical light
we listened to the sea in conch shells
and held fragile sand dollars in our palms
Then we paid admission to cross behind
a wooden fence to watch the Seminole
He dressed in a colorful striped shirt
and used a bullhorn to inform the tourists
what his opponent was like in the wild
Day after day he went through a routine
he flipped the lethargic beast onto its back
and feigned caution as he rubbed its belly
Centuries of survival in the everglades
reduced to this ritual for the tourists
released for a week or two
from their own empty routines
Driving back to Detroit my father would sigh
You just start to unwind
then you have to go back to work
He made tiny parts for nuclear missiles
the family lived with his chronic sadness
With only the money for gas to get home
my mother would fret and cry out
I'm sick of this, I'm sick of not having money
Once she tore her dress from her bosom
I'm sick of my old clothes
The sight of her white lace slip scared us
she leaned her head against the car window
and we were all silent for the rest of the trip

While Gardening, I Remember a Dream

I sift the black earth
through my fingers
darkness to which we all return
the musk releases a mystery
I imagine the emergence
of delicate green shoots
While gardening, I remember a dream
I visit my Polish grandmother
she lives in a white, shingled house
we move through the dim, musty rooms
to the screen of the back door
out back there is a garden
The earth is dark and rich
a high, wooden fence
surrounds the garden
the earth has been turned over
green shoots emerge in the rows
As I admire the garden
I hear the click of a lock
a laugh from my grandmother
the screen door has been locked
she has withdrawn into the house
Above the fence I see
the sky turning orange and pink
the sun sinking fast
There's no way out
only the darkness of the earth
only the fragrance of the earth

Primal Dream

In the aftermath of a tornado
my sister and I wander in the rubble
looking for our parents, our brothers
finally in an old section of the city
we find my grandmother's first house
it is the house of an immigrant
no glass in the windows
light and wind pass through
cracks in the floor and walls
doors hang off their hinges
The walls are not flush
and there are mouse droppings
all over the linoleum floors
I have nowhere to put things
nowhere to sleep, no bed or dresser
I search down the basement
and find a pile of my clothing
on the rank earth floor
a hot wind blows through a window
my clothes ignite in flames
Even rags under the sink
can cause a fire
as my mother would say
In the yard there is a plum tree
all the fruit has dropped to the ground
over-sized and mushy, inedible
If she were still alive
the fruit would be picked and frozen
When I go back in the house
I almost fall though a patchwork
of plywood and old linoleum
I ask my sister if she wants to leave
so we can find another place to live
To stay would be to eat the eel
served on the night before Easter
but she is resigned to stay and wait

continued

I can't take any more of this!
My spirit turns into a dust devil
Wait till I slash my wrists!
I scream to anyone
who may be hiding in a closet
or down in the basement

West

The Hitch-hiker

For hours he'd been waiting
praying for a ride
on the road outside of Mission
His hair is half-tucked
into an old stocking cap
his surplus army coat
doubles as a blanket
Over and over he thanks us
as we drive towards Nebraska
where he can spend the night
by the Niobrara River
"Moccasin Face" is his name
he writes poetry
I asked Him to teach me
all about writing
so I could spread the Word
Do you know God
in your own way?
Once he worked in a factory
he still has bits of metal
lodged in eyes glazed
with divinity and alcohol
Now he writes about his travels
and tries to recite from memory
Counting the cracks
in the highway
I fear the coming night
That is all he remembers
but promises to send more
on each copy we will find
his fingerprint, a copyright
He looks anxiously for deer
that may have retreated
to higher ground
escaping the spring snow

continued

By the side of the Niobrara
golden in the dusk
and free of ice
we leave Moccasin Face
He will settle into her
as he would a lover
and eat in the morning
at an all-night truck stop
If you listen to the river
it will tell you its history
Do you know God
in your own way?

Paying Attention

The first *mni wozon*
cold rain falls on sage
that has gone to seed
and the shriveled rose hips
The woman of the house has prayed
a relative has brought a gift of meat
The windows are opaque
with steam from the soup
Crow Dog speaks

   We're getting soft-headed
   this white man's food
   sugar and cholesterol
   waste sni
   We're not paying attention
   last year you saw
   chokecherries and plums
   this year—nothing sweet
   We're not going by the cycles
   Wagluhtatapisni
   But there's a lot of sage
    that's a warning
   We're supposed to pick that sage
    purify ourselves and start over
    At the tribal building
    I see an *iyeska* and Lakota
    they fight with their fists
    over who's Indian, who's not
    The government has all that paper
    Let's see: how much Indian
    blood is in your veins?
   We should have burned those papers!
   Red Cloud and Spotted Tail

continued

they were ready to march
us all down to Oklahoma
Then the agents said:
You can stay: no minerals
We don't want this land
There's nothing
If we get the Black Hills back
the government will say:
You owe us
They'll tax this land
If we can't pay
they'll take it away
Termination
We've got to pay attention

Who could look at this prairie
a perfect orchestration
of sumac and yucca
sage and sunflowers
and see *nothing*
Here a few pounds of meat
some potatoes, carrots, and squash
are enough to feed
a circle of relatives

mni wozon – a cold, steady rain
waste sni – this isn't good
wagluhtatapisni – offerings are not being made
iyeska – a mixed-blood Indian

Thinning the Herd

Your children cherish the two colts
but the winter has been tough
snow has been falling since October
and after the summer drought
hay is scarce and expensive
Then there's the cost of electricity
and the prospect of the funeral
with your father's death imminent
So the two colts will be sold
for fifty dollars and enough hay
to feed the mares already with foal
Besides the Larvies are good with horses
and their whole herd was stolen last spring

You call the herd into the corral
the pink-nosed stallion is incensed
when the gate shuts him off from the rest
The mares and colts expect trouble
tails turned up, their legs churn
and mix the black earth with the snow
Like a sleepwalker your daughter
stands near the shed holding a brush
The sons of the Larvies
eye their colts with pride
Your son sits on the roof of the shed
and throws snowballs
You say: *There'll be other horses*
We'd have to buy more hay
wouldn't we? he answers

A fog is rolling in from the east
in this whiteness the barn is a red ship
the trees in the break are dark and wet

continued

When the mares are caught and led away
they cry out and dance in fear
The Larvie brothers are so good with horses
there is a fierce will and love in their eyes
with the grace of birds they spread their arms
and *plie;* cornered the colts
trip up into the horse trailer

The boys laugh; your son throws a snowball
the Larvie men ask about names and birth dates
The mares can sense the loss
we hear their grief as the trailer pulls out
You say it will take days for them to dry
their milk will leak out on the snow as they walk
You wonder if the corral can contain them
and share a story about two mares
who broke several fences and ran five miles
to be reunited with their colts
so strong is the bond between them
Your son is congratulated
he has given away the colts without tears
He said: *There'll be other horses*

In the house we warm ourselves with tea
and listen for the pair of horned owls
which make their nest in the break
and call to one another in the evening
swooping low over the grass behind the barn
You plan a trip to visit your father
What can be said in the end?
The seam between snow and sky disappears
the remaining corn and telephone poles
are sharp etchings in this mute whiteness
I would like to lose all substance
and come out of the fog like a spotted eagle
and wrap a quilt of consolation around you

Heart of Clover

A freak April storm
has whitened the East
We saw images on tv
of tree blossoms heavy with ice
You were lying on the couch
in a square of sunlight
I have ten acres of apple trees
in upstate New York
you said in a dream
In summer I go there
and give the apples to hunters
I bit into your words
In the front yard two piles
of rotting walnuts
fragrant and mealy
were covered by clover
a rare green in the snow melt
I became a hunter
with a heart of clover
tracing a river to its source

Picking Tea in Grass Mountain

July is the best time
to pick the tea
before the purple flowers
return to seed
Rubbed between the fingers
the leaves smell like
lemon, mint, and lavender
they are flecked with gold
Rita needs ten bundles
for all of the Sun Dancers
meeting in August
down at Big Mountain
Thinning out the clumps of tea
that grow around the home-site
we despair: the earth is ravaged
to satisfy the urges of a few
This house will be made
from earth, straw, and wood

The men prepare the fire
for the sweat lodge
the stones are dropped
our prayers spread in circles
Afterwards we languish
in the White River
I lose all substance
and let the current take me
My hands search for sharp edges
some rocks are smooth and flat
beneath my body
In a deep, sandy hollow
I grab a root and remain
quiet as a lily
I could stay all evening
the sky turning rose
above the steep banks
the young coyotes
crying to one another

Lament for the Waning Female Moons

In the old days it was like this:
the women knew the language of the moon
wild sweet potatoes and squash were gathered
at a precise time and place
only enough for the need was taken
and an offering was left behind
The branches of the plum tree
were never broken
When snow was still on the ground
the women walked along the creeks
and when they felt a hump in the earth
beneath their moccasins
the women dug for the nests of field mice
there wild beans were stored
tallow fat was left for the relatives
In the beginning: how did the women learn?
The grandmothers shrug and sip their coffee
each day their faces reach closer to the earth
like the darkened faces of the sunflowers
When the winter solstice comes
there will be another cluster of wakes
and still there is so much to be learned

Alice Fish at a Rosebud *Wacipi*

The folds in her skin are deep
as those in a walnut
the contours of her face
like the plains
shaped over many years
She keeps time with her cane
at the July 4th *wacipi*
and braces her scarf
against the hot and steady wind
How many of them are there?
she asks for each event
men's fancy, women's traditional
and squints into the arena
where ribbons, shawl fringe, and feathers
move like weeds beneath the water
The white film on her eyes
is spreading like algae in late summer
She laughs when a fancy dancer
in black and white feathers
continues his step after
the last beat of the drum
And when Blue Thunder donates
money to a singing group
She asks, *How much? Twenty dollars?*
when in fact it was ten
Her heart aligns itself with the drum
she shuffles to the end of the shade
and rocks gently from leg to leg
The call of the eagle
is still strong in her throat
And then she waves her arm
as though she has finally
traveled through the Milky Way
and has reached the hill where

continued

below the camp named after
the wild pink rosebud appears
and her relatives greet her
lead her to a teepee
where a set of clothing waits
Alice hears them singing
as they prepare the feast

wacipi – pow-wow

Gladys Makes Room for Them Crosses Over

Her dress was the color
of a late evening storm
it was studded with shells
and pinned to the back
a red chiffon scarf
floated in the breeze
For many years she had competed
with the older, traditional dancers
but this year she lacked vigor
and slowed like a lead bird
rotating to the back of the flock
Those watching the other dancers
or visiting with friends
did not see her sudden drop
but turned their attention
to the center of the arbor
when the drums abruptly stopped
A siren filled the vacuum
from an aisle in the shade
a relative ran and cried
That's grandmother
He stopped to turn away
the faces of the children
then a wave of grief
took him into the circle

When the rocks are ready
for the sweat lodge
the wood falls easily away
the ceremony can begin
The medics weren't needed
the *eyapaha* announced
Gladys Makes Room For Them
has crossed to the other side

There was a mourning song
four dancers each held
the corner of a star quilt
and slowly made an orbit
coins and dollars were tossed
some shook the hands of her relatives

A year later at the *wacipi*
a memorial was held
and the competing dancers
were asked to come forward
for a piece of the cake
that was baked in her honor

eyapaha – announcer at a pow-wow

Somehow We Managed

In the morning she awoke to the sound
of her mother's pounding rock
and the tart smell of choke cherries
Somehow we managed to get by
before the checks made it easy
Always there was work to be done
and there was a rhythm to life
In late June the turnips were ready
when the berries were dark in August
they'd travel by wagon to the Niabrara
where the bushes were heavy with fruit
By summer's end the clothes line would droop
with strips of squash and meat dried by the sun
Somehow they managed to get a beef
and then they dried that for the long winter
On cold days they'd boil the hooves for hours
this made a rich broth and kept the house warm
The muscle that came loose was a delicacy
and the bones could be made into a toy horse
We Lakota like that dark green squash
to this day I grow some in my yard
and I keep in mind lady friends
who don't have a plot of land
or are unable to dig at their age
I took one out to the yard one spring night
the moon was out, and oh!
those yellow blossoms!
"Look," I said, "how pretty they are…
this summer we'll be drying squash"

Agnes, Trying to Stay Sober

The men have started to drink again
but Agnes is trying to stay sober
her brother came home with that woman
who pawned the radio for a pint
The old man spent his whole check
so Agnes hid her good dishes in the attic

>*Agnes, you want a drink?* they ask
>I try to concentrate on my beading
>but when they're drunk they cry around
>I said: *If you're going to drink*
>*you should at least be happy*
>Then they couldn't stop laughing

When it's warm, Agnes goes to the old place
out on the prairie she can pick berries
There is peace there, birds in the morning
she can't understand why the white man
built the new housing in clusters

>I go to the pow-wows
>just to sell my berries
>I keep to myself
>I used to dance
>when I was nine
>I won $50 in a contest
>I heard all those people clapping
>and ran behind my grandma's skirts

Agnes once went on the road with Roy Rogers
she would dance three times a day
and take in the carnival rides for free
Flicker would dance for the crowd
and count out his years with one hoof

continued

> My grandmother made coffee
> and soup in huge pots
> By the end of the tour
> we had lots of money
> I'd have a new pair of shoes
> each month of the winter

When the men sell the commodities
they all have to go hungry
Agnes is looking for another place
but she needs an increase in G.A.

> Now Roy Rogers is dead
> and I think white people
> would rather complain
> about these checks we get
> than to pay to see us dance

Dreams in a Season of Drought

The cicadas sing
the earth turns to dust
Clouds pass around us
to the east or south
the prairie is on fire
on and off the sirens pull
exhausted crews to new fires
thousands of acres are charred
a preview of the apocalypse
There is dust on my table
the counter of my sink
my own house looks abandoned
At night I cool
as slowly as a rock

In this fever I dream
my first child is born
but I leave to work
when I turn back
it is too late
the child rises and moves away
pale as the moon
viewed in the early evening sky
I find three old women
wise and aloof
waiting for me in my home
their hair is twisted into plumes
finally they ask
if I need medicine
I am in a lush garden
every plant is over-sized
at the perimeters

continued

there is scorched earth
I find small crystals
placed here and there
in the greenery
a mirror of star patterns

There are low-lying areas
on the prairie
near the aquifers
which are still dark green
and thick with wild flowers
blackbirds and larks stay there
once I saw a blue crane
Even as the higher grounds erode
such places remain fresh and wet
as the inside of a melon
cold as the spring water
deep in a sun-warmed lake
When it finally rains
the sunflowers will double
in the course of a day

In Honor of the *Wakinyan Oyate*

When the *wakinyan oyate* claim a soul
that person must live out the vision
dance on the plains, dance alone
when the terrible and powerful nation
returns after a long, Dakota winter
At the Sun Dance a man is blind-folded
a lightning bolt decorates his skirt
He has set himself apart from the others
he dances with his back to the tree
and holds his pipe upside down
honoring the terrible and powerful nation
Others have been chased down from the hill
dodging tongues of lightning
a parachute of a star quilt behind them

Last summer the *wakinyan oyate*
set the Black Hills on fire
and drove residents away in anguish
over lost property and trade
The sun reached the floor of the forest
grass and shrubs began to grow
water swelled in the streams
elk and buffalo reclaimed their home
When the first thunder is heard in the spring
the *heyoka* dance alone on the plains
the old people still tell stories
about the days when warriors
still battled with the lightning
shooting their arrows into the sky
challenging the terrible and powerful nation

wakinyan oyate – Thunder Nation
heyoka – "contrary" person who has had a vision of the Thunder Nation

On the Fourth Day

This was the summer the farms
in East Dakota were flooded out
The weather had been good
for the Ring Thunder *wacipi*
until late on the fourth day
The flag had been lowered
and the vets had danced
to an honoring song
Then from the west
the clouds rolled in dark blue
and dense as the old buffalo herds
But still the drumming continued
some folded up their chairs
and took refuge in cars
Dust was thrown high by the wind
feather bustles were strained
and the dancers began to remove
roach pieces and chokers
Then in large drops the rain
came smelling of pine
A drum was hurried
to the back of a pick-up
a breast plate folded
into an open suitcase
But still the drumming continued
Spring Creek played on
and one young woman
in a white shawl
took the form of a crane
and flapped alone in the arbor
Then an older man dressed
in an army jacket and baseball cap
joined her and danced

continued

for the first time that year
He felt his spirit rise
like the nearby White River
Later there was a lightning storm
and for those who were left
the electric rivers and tributaries
of the sky were made visible

Dream of Purification

There has been a great storm or flood
the earth has been purified
I am back in Dakota
there are lakes
in the hollows of the plains
The sky is a stormy, purple-blue
and I realize
It will always be evening now
Overhead is a cloud shaped like a buffalo
I am reminded of *Tayamni*
a Lakota constellation
The cloud opens and stars fall out
when they reach the earth
they are iridescent flakes
I am back at a friend's house
a white frame farm house
isolated on the prairie
I hear voices and laughter outside
All my friends are returning
they are arriving for this reunion
 I embrace my friend
and then I understand
There is no flesh between us
Her children come into the room
screaming with excitement
we look at the screen door
a large, black bat
has fastened itself there
We all cry out and our cries
are a mixture of terror and joy
In another room is a table
radishes, beets, and green beans are there
they are delicate and precious
and then I realize
This is our very first harvest

Beyond

Locating Myself in Space and Time

West of Mt. Taylor
shadowed facets the color of coal
snow-capped and heavenly after a storm
Twenty thousand years have passed
since the last eruption
when elk stood under the same stars
to view the molten lava
hardening near the land where
the people of Acoma later settled
Their orchards bloom year after year

North of Cibola Forest
where potsherds blend with quartz
sandstone and petrified wood
fragments of cooking jars
grey and corrugated
bowls with geometric designs
red ware and kiva jars
evidence of trade
through the Chaco center
I find fingerprints in the clay
and feel the pulse and breath
of the people who grew corn
on the flats along the arroyo
under the same turquoise sky
Same blue birds, same smoke from pinon

East of the desert canyon and mesas
where the Hopi settled after the clans
returned from their migrations
to the ends of the continent and back
finally home on their high, arid plateau
where the ancient dances

continued

must be remembered and performed
for the earth to stay in balance
The kachinas return to the white peaks
of the San Francisco mountains
after they dance in the villages

South of the red rock mesas
where the play of light
signals the time of day or season
As the sun rises in the late morning
images emerge from the shadows
a Mayan temple, skull of a deer
faces of the original ones
and the letters of their alphabet
Near sunset the red rocks burn
with the light of molten lava
as they always have

I locate myself in space and time
between the four Sacred Mountains
close to the rift where the continent divides
All rivers to the east
flow to the Atlantic
All rivers to the west
flow to the Pacific
The cold, thin air of the Rockies
flows down from the north
Bird songs and the hum of insects
drift faintly up from the south
and I am in rapture with those
who have always lived on this continent

Spirit of the Horse

From a distance I spot
the great ivory ribs
arching over the desert scrub
the remains of a horse
under a tall pinon tree
I approach with trepidation
dreading scavengers and rot
but coyotes have picked it clean
inside the chest cavity
there is a great void
The skull of the horse
burrows into the earth
the cream-colored tail is still intact
and part of the hide on the flank
of this brown and white Appaloosa
now lifeless as dried wood
I call to the spirit of the horse
Where did you go?
With the motion and grace of clouds
did you head toward Mt. Taylor in the east?
Or were you drawn to the west
by the San Francisco peaks?
Come back!
These bones and hair are nothing
without you

Circle of Wildness

I follow the path
of two coyotes
Fresh in the snow
their tracks run parallel
almost touch at points
then veer apart
The coyotes may have
traveled together
in the arroyo
or followed one another
under the highway
to the wilderness beyond
One of the trails
cuts close to the edge
of the canyon
I follow until I see
the ledge is precarious
and I'm not as well-balanced
or light as the coyote
The other tracks cut up
a rocky slope to a mesa
but I'm not as sure-footed
or able to withstand the cold
as the coyote
I am the first human
to tread the virgin snow
the sage is sharply etched
pinon and juniper dark green
I walk deeper
deeper into the desert wilderness
I sense the coyotes watching me
I enter their circle of wildness
if I don't turn back now
I may never return

Meditations on Water in the Desert

On the other side of the fence
the wild horses drink
from the artesian spring
necks arched they keep
the lush greenery clipped
The water is a gift
I stand with a hose
watering corn already
dry and spindly
the seeds are Midwestern
almost useless here
How long will it take
before I take root in this soil?

How do the Hopi grow corn
high on their desert plateau?
Green sprouts thrive in sand
while the water resides
in springs beneath the rock
During the Niman kachina
the bounty of the pueblo
is spread out in the square
corns, melons, squash
Draped in pine boughs
and eagle feathers
the dancers pass out the harvest
while the tortoise shells
strapped to their legs
tap out a rhythm which
resonates in the stars or deep
within the core of the earth

continued

I climb from the desert
to the high lands
of Lukachukai
on a pilgrimage
to a mountain spring
There is the sound
of pick-ups changing gears
A cascade of water
emerges from the rock
people come with containers
to take water home
or stand and cup their hands
let the water wash over their heads
or into their mouths
a blessing
At night there is a storm
but it is fine red sand
not water
that blows across the desert
until the hogans are barely visible

The desert leaves me hollow
dry and light
as the bones of an eagle
In my dreams
I begin my migrations
I descend to aquifers
I cross the desert to the ocean
I reach the glaciers in the mountains
restored I return to the light
to the pinon and yucca and sage
to all living things
which live on a vision of water

Exhumation of Florence C. Lister, author of *Anasazi Pottery*

She coveted Anasazi pots
she begged for them
paid the Navajo
as little as she could
She approached the widow
of a man who wouldn't sell
during his lifetime
Her father broke into
a burial room near Farmington
where bodies lay three deep
and she continued his work
traveling around the Four Corners
in the 20's and 30's
She competed with other Sunday diggers
for the pots in the ancient ruins
but she felt "no compunction"
for she could not imagine
the pots in "their" hands

When she thrust her shovel in a mound
and uncovered human ribs
her heart raced with excitement
the possibility of more pots!
After only a few minutes work
I found the burial of a child
but there remained only
the disintegrated bones—
no pottery whatsoever

continued

Those were beautiful pots
you collected, Florence
but you are still just a gravedigger
so I am going to exhume your body
and take special note
of the artifacts buried with you
perhaps a crucifix
and I am going to measure
the size of your skull
to determine
if you were truly human
or if you were more closely related
to our less evolved ancestors

For who could be so crass
as to violate human graves
in order to hoard the ceramic pots
the dead would need
in their travels to the next world?

Visit to a Chaco Canyon Excavation

To make way for a gas pipeline
the team has been charged
to exhume and rebury human remains
from what once was a settlement of Chaco
The desert has been tiered and squared
into an archeological grid
small flags serve as markers
paper bags are filled with pot sherds, tools
The team avoids the nearby hogan
a burial place for a Navajo
The walls and floors of a kiva
are emerging from the earth
the team studies a jumble of bones
discarded in a corner, some knawed
the marrow extracted in others
they suspect cannibalism
One man holds a femur and jokes
Man does not live by corn alone
I try to impose my Western grid
What about wild animals?
a massacre from a hostile tribe?
drought and desperation?
-No. These people ate each other
They shake their heads and check
the skies for afternoon storms
The Navajo experience pain in the legs
if they step over Anasazi bones
and must have a sing later in life
to restore balance in their lives
At night, one archeologist in camp
will turn on a friend
drunk and delirious from the sun
he will say: *It was you!*
You who ate those bodies 500 years ago!
Some man will laugh, another turn in early
and each will wish he had brought a knife

A Storm, A Dream

Magnificent and dark blue
the storm moves to the south
a tongue of lightning
strikes from its heart
The wet, red earth
around the Continental Divide
has the texture and muscle
of a bobcat's fur
the sage is a deeper green
In a valley near the red rocks
the light arcs into
a full spectrum of color
As the sun drops below the
 western canopy of clouds
the high, rolling desert
is diffused with sudden gold

In my dream
I am with you again
and move toward you
like the spring run of water
from the Sangre de Christos
into the rivers, arroyos, and desert
I awake replenished
I walk toward the rainbow
in the valley near the red rocks
but it recedes into the distance
I know you will only be with me
when the conditions
of the sky are right
an intense arc of colors
an illusion

Land-owner

The borders of the land
are still pristine
I follow deer tracks
and marvel over the compact
between yucca and cactus
cedar wood dry as bone
the architecture of stairs
made from flat stones
The silence is in my ears
like the wings of insects
now I can hear the surf of my blood

The inner section of the land
has been cleared—weeds rage
but on the borders
the earth exudes moisture
and I am as thirsty for water
as the shallow roots of the pinon
I want to know as the Anasazi did
how to get to the nearest spring
how many nights I could keep warm
by burning this dried wood

I traveled to the Tetons years ago
with my Lakota companion
Weary, we scouted for a public space
where we could camp and rest
Public lands were being sold off
we followed the fence lines
prohibiting us from meadows and forests
warning signs: NO TRESPASSING

continued

See what this country has become?
my friend railed as we left
the remote Tetons in our rear-view mirror
and searched for a cheap motel
I imagined vacation homes for the elite
with cathedral ceilings and huge logs
stripped from the old forests of the Northwest
PRIVATE PROPERTY: KEEP OUT

A mountain side becomes a site
for a new ski lodge
a cave: a tomb for waste
a plain: a factory for beef
a territory: a source of rancor
borders marked with blood
What is this paper deed
easements and mineral rights
assigned to the developers
xerox copies in offices
a military to protect what is now
under this government "mine"?

Below in the distance I see lights
the silent passage of the Sante Fe
at the base of the darkening mesa
The coyotes can hear the train
feel the vibrations in the earth
they begin to yelp in response
With all the dried wood here
I could build a fire: I feel safe

We Create Myth

On the way to the ranch
the road curved through territory
Billy the Kid once roamed
when I saw the man
naked he walked across the desert
his car abandoned behind him
I strained to see a remnant of dress
he wore tennis shoes, had a beard
luminous white and free he strode
a sight as rare as cactus
coming at last into flower

Did you see him?
Did you see that man?
He was completely naked
just walking out there
You didn't see him
Are you sure?
No other cars were on the road
Yes. I'm sure that's what I saw
a naked man walking out there
You laughed: we did not turn back

Born in the wrong century
you would have hung out with the Kid
who knew about greed
how politicians and businessmen
warm their feet under the same quilt
You're no fool: love adventure
almost made it to the Finals in Vegas
From the age of two
you could make a rocking horse
move clear across the room
fed your imaginary horse oats
before you ate your own

continued

Your grandparents' ranch
with its view of Mt. Blanca
was part of a Spanish land grant
but Mexicans were not allowed
the land near the river
It takes a large herd of sheep
and sweat to endure on this arid soil
Horses have to be raised here
so their muscles and hooves
adapt to the rocky hills
Your grandparents are gnarled
and sturdy as old saguaros
Can you imagine seventy years
with the same battle-ax?
your grandfather complains
I tried to leave once…
Yes, his wife responds
he packed his suitcase
put it there by the door
but I picked it up
I wouldn't let him go

The sight of Mt. Blanca's peaks
rarified by snow: my spirit
could feed on this vision
until the sun engulfs the earth
The naked man now reminds me
of the Spanish explorer
Cabeza De Vaca Nunez
Hungry and naked
he continued his adventures
in the "unknown interior"
surviving on the prickly pear
plentiful on the desert floor

continued

We ate not more than two handfuls
of prickly pears a day
and they were still so green and milky
they burned our mouths
I am tempted to taste them
to take my off my clothes, eat prickly pear
and gaze at the snow peaks of Mt. Blanca

The lambs startle at the sound
as the pellets are poured in the feeder
Wear Wool—Eat Lamb declares
the bumper sticker on the pick-up
Without the subsidies, who knows?
We survey the stone remains
of the very first house
the simple shack where
most of the children were born
The arroyo is filled with busted tv's
lame bikes and such
a dead calf by the stock pond
was worth four hundred bucks
the ranch can support a family: no more
At ninety your grandfather laments
I had nine sons and now
there is no one to work the ranch

I am an explorer in this desert
my relatives were peasants in Europe
here factory workers and coal miners
I want to visit the cliff in Acoma
from which an arrogant priest was hurled
I want to love a man
who was born in the wrong century
listen to his grandparents

continued

gossip about me in Spanish
I want to hear the audible cries
coming from a statue of the Virgin
hidden from Protestants
in the back room of a home in Laguna
Then I can add my own story
about a man who abandoned his car
to walk naked across the desert

Love at Mid-Life

A year ago on this land
where I would build my house
I scattered the seeds
of sunflowers
not knowing if they would grow
More than a ritual
with rain the flowers grew
some to ten feet
through clay they bloomed
where only rocks reside
they broke through the soil

Under their own weight
they droop like monks
and the birds arrive
they know
they know what will come
Drops of water on the leaves
dry when the sun tops the trees
Under the earth the roots connect
and make a basket for my home

In the back are two trees
one living, and one dead
the red mesa beyond
was once under a sea
For years I was dry
ready for the woodpile
then you arrived
a comet in the night sky
and I turned to the spruce

July: your people dance
on a mesa to the west
*Do the men dance the rain down
or honor the monsoon?*

continued

I am here without songs
to seduce corn from the earth
without memories
of volcanic eruptions
The same power that turns
the flowers to the sun
turns me to you
Forgive my short tenure
when you come

The first time
you took a full minute
and your cries cut through
rock with the fury of
all water released
from the beginning in
 the creation of rivers
And the last time
I remember the outline
of your body
usually solid as earth
turned to waves of light
I saw your face
in atoms of color
I closed my eyes
and understood
what lamas call
rainbow body

Do you know
there is a tear of flesh
under your eye
like one on a sculpture
of a saint?
And look at my body:
glyphs on my arms and legs

continued

the last light of a dying star
in my uterus
my heart drying
a used honeycomb

Here: you left black hair
on my pillow
broken strings of a violin
should I keep it
with my son's baby teeth?

Faces to the earth
the sunflowers dry
dark and beautiful
as the Inca girl
found on a mountain
with an ax in her skull

Before you left my home
you lingered for a moment
and noted two piles of wood
Do you remember the time
I asked you to make a fire?
*Haven't you made a fire
since I was here last?*
Ah, love: if I had waited
I would be so cold

Ordained you stayed
for nights like a comet
I'll keep my eyes on the earth
near the divide of the continent
if I see you again
it will be by mere fortune

Continental Divide

What separates us?
40 miles and a ridge
Should I come over?
Snow falls
this could be a sign
or a curtain
I see your shadow
There might be black ice
Let's see: Milan, Grants
Is it still coming down?
I am warm
but need wood
your brother has a saw
but his house is cold
The water from my place
flows to the west
the water from your place
flows to the east
But look at the globe
marbled with water
more water than earth
All rivers empty
all water converges
We are more water
than we are earth

The Return of Odysseus

In this dream
I am back in the city
where I grew up
boxed in an apartment
I hear the sound of cars
voices and music
What happened to the beauty
of the West in my life?
There is someone at the door
and before I reach for the lock
my old lover is inside
dressed for a wedding
But this is unexpected
he is all of the lovers
who have come in
and out of my life
I look across the street
there is a pueblo-style church
the doors are open
people wait for a ceremony
When I turn to my lover
he has slipped into my bed
a guileless smile on his face
Odysseus, your return
is darkly comic
I am shamed by
the mix of fear and desire
but my roots hold water
In the desert of the West
the waters of my sleep
are so clear
I can see the very bottom
I have not traveled far
from myself

Holy Rain

After four years of drought
sand bars emerging from the Rio Grande
forest fires starting in May
a deluge began during Holy Week
on the very day my guests and I
drove the back roads to Chimayo
In Mora people left town when
water reached the bellies of their cattle
As the temperature dropped
the rain turned to slush, then hail
How beautiful the desert looked
white pearls between greening sage
rivulets of silver water over rock and clay
water pooled near the sides of the road
washes filled and rivers too, finally

> *In this vastness our vehicles are shells*
> *in low areas we fear wash outs*
> *all we can do is continue breathing in*
> *the newly-released smells of the desert*
> *As we approach the town of Coyote*
> *there is an explosion in the sky*
> *white and almost nuclear*
> *rods of lightning appear for an instant*
> *Sober, we are too close to this power*

As we drove I tried to explain
how the Spanish coveted the land
the revolt of the Pueblo people
running with their knotted rope
to tell others of the exact date
they would drive the Spanish away
And how on their return ten years later
they coerced the Pueblo to haul
heavy vigas from Mt. Taylor
to their mission church in Acoma

continued

My guests marveled at the hogans
we passed from time to time
the smoke from wood-burning stoves
in the mobile homes beyond Cuba

> *Such comfort to arrive at the Inn*
> *with its walls of earth two-feet thick*
> *built in 1700 for travelers who*
> *must have crossed themselves*
> *as the flicker of candles came to view*
> *I run my hands over the uneven roll*
> *of the plastered wall, note the craft*
> *and imperfections of the wood doors*
> *In this place where we will sleep*
> *men have died, women gave birth*
> *and couples muffled cries of love*
> *to spare the ears of other guests*

In the Sanctuario de Chimayo
devotions to Mary are underway
the passion of the Spanish songs
is full and rolling as the rivers
The altar paintings in primary colors
are primitive in hand but full of heart
statues of Mary and the saints tremor
I close my eyes and see a forest of candles
At this moment I forgive the Spanish
vexed by our wickedness and divinity
I wonder how rain can bring
both calamity and holiness

Gathering Poles at Quaking Aspens

Gathering poles for my coyote fence
I bend the leafless aspens, once gold
some break easily; these I take
But where there is pliancy in wood
there is still life, another winter
I leave these, and strip away the bark
from those poles scorched in a fire
to find the secret work of insects
An ocean sound moves the forest
soon ice and wind will loosen roots

Twenty poles from Quaking Aspens
make for two feet of fence
each year my roots loosen
In the stillness of practice
the bow of my spine is pliant
I travel in a vessel
made of paper and wood

> *There were four Buddhas*
> *in my dream*
> *three had faces veiled by silk*
> *One was prone, ready for birth*
> *his carved ivory skin worn*
> *through centuries was like the*
> *wood stripped of its bark*
> *to reveal the secret glyphs of being*

I hear the coyotes taunting the dogs
as they pass through the arroyo;
the days shorten, the cries come earlier
I fasten pole to pole with baling wire
the fence wouldn't keep coyotes out
but I have nothing to protect:
the practice is my winter count

continued

When the moon unravels itself from the clouds
and floats on the clear lake of space
I imagine *this is how it will be in the end*
a brightening of a candle in a paper lantern
and then a darkness lighter than light

About the Author

Gloria Dyc was on the editorial board of *Moving Out*, the Detroit-based feminist literary journal in the 1970's; she was also involved in the Cass Corridor literary and arts scene. In 1982 she moved to the Rosebud Reservation in South Dakota to teach at Sinte Gleska University. The Lakota generously shared their culture and ceremonies. Dyc was an editor of *Wanbli Ho*, and helped to bring native writers to the college. In 1988 she relocated to New Mexico to teach at the University of New Mexico-Gallup where she is now a full professor. Dyc is on the editorial board of the award-winning college journal *The Red Mesa Review*, and has facilitated readings by Native American poets.

Gloria Dyc has also published fiction; in 1981 she won a major Hopwood Award in Fiction at the University of Michigan where she earned her Doctor of Arts in English Language and Literature. Her fiction has appeared in *yefief*, *The Sun*, *Short Fiction by Women*, *Sing! Heavenly Muse*, *Moving Out*, *Seven Hundred Kisses: A Yellow Silk Book of Erotic Writing*, *Southwestern Women: New Voices* , and others.

She continues to explore the alchemy of consciousness in the Zuni Mountain sangha of the Vairotsana Foundation, under the direction of Tibetan lamas in exile.

www.ingramcontent.com/pod-product-compliance
Lightning Source LLC
Chambersburg PA
CBHW070119110526
44587CB00015BA/2565